I Like Biographies!

Read About
Cesar Chavez

Stephen Feinstein

Enslow Publishers, Inc.

40 Industrial Road	PO Box 38
Box 398	Aldershot
Berkeley Heights, NJ 07922	Hants GU12 6BP
USA	UK

http://www.enslow.com

Words to Know

crops—Fruits and vegetables growing in the field.

farm workers—People who take care of the crops and pick them.

migrants—People who move from place to place.

union—A group of workers who fight for their rights.

Library of Congress Cataloging-in-Publication Data

Feinstein, Stephen.
    Read about Cesar Chavez / Stephen Feinstein.— 1st ed.
        v. cm. — (I like biographies!)
    Includes bibliographical references and index.
    Contents: Growing up on a farm—Hard work for the family—Helping farm workers—Making a union—Timeline—Learn more.
    ISBN 0-7660-2296-X
    1. Chavez, Cesar, 1927—Juvenile literature. 2. Mexican American migrant agricultural laborers—Biography—Juvenile literature. 3. Migrant agricultural laborers—Labor unions—United States—History—Juvenile literature. 4. Mexican Americans—Biography—Juvenile literature. [1. Chavez, Cesar, 1927– 2. Labor leaders. 3. Migrant labor. 4. United Farm Workers. 5. Mexican Americans—Biography.] I. Title. II. Series.
    HD6509.C48F44 2004
    331.88'13'092—dc22
                                        2003022124

Printed in the United States of America

10 9 8 7 6 5 4 3 2 1

To Our Readers: We have done our best to make sure all Internet Addresses in this book were active and appropriate when we went to press. However, the author and the publisher have no control over and assume no liability for the material available on those Internet sites or on links to other Web sites. Any comments or suggestions can be sent by e-mail to comments@enslow.com or to the address on the back cover.

Illustration Credits: AP/Wide World, pp. 1, 3, 13, 21; © Bettmann/Corbis, p. 17; Cesar E. Chavez Foundation, p. 5; Walter P. Reuther Library, Wayne State University, pp. 7, 9, 11, 15, 19.

Cover Illustration: Arthur Schatz/Getty Images.

Contents

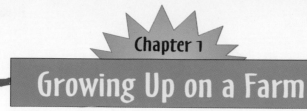

Cesar Chavez was born in Arizona on March 31, 1927. He grew up on his family's farm.

Cesar's grandfather was a poor farmer in Mexico. He came north looking for a better life in the United States.

Cesar was one of six children. Here he is with his older sister, Rita, at their First Communion.

Cesar's grandfather bought a farm. He grew crops on the farm. The Chavez family paid workers to help them pick the crops. The farm workers moved from job to job. They were called migrant farm workers.

Migrant workers had to bend over to hoe crops in the fields.

In 1937, Cesar was ten years old. It did not rain much that year. Crops did not grow. Cesar's father could not pay his bills. So the Chavez family lost their farm. They had nothing but an old car. Farm work was the only work they could do.

Cesar graduated from eighth grade in 1942. He was fifteen.

9

In the fall, the Chavez family became migrant farm workers too. They picked vegetables and fruits. They moved from farm to farm in California. Sometimes they had to sleep in their car. Sometimes they stayed in work camps. The camps were not clean.

Camps for migrant workers were dirty.

Life was very hard. Even the children had to work picking fruit or vegetables. Workers got paid for each box they filled. It took a long time to fill a box with fruit. They made only a few cents a day. The farm owners did not care.

This ten-year-old girl is picking grapes and putting them on paper to dry.

Cesar wanted to help migrant farm workers. But he did not know what to do. Other workers came together in unions to fight for their rights. But farm workers could not do this.

In 1945, Cesar went into the Navy. He got out in 1948. Then he went back to work in the fields.

Cesar married Helen Fabela in 1948. Later they had eight children. Three of their girls are shown here.

In 1952, Cesar met Fred Ross. Ross worked for the Community Service Organization, or CSO. Cesar helped Ross to get the workers together. Ross showed the workers how to vote. He showed them how to fight for their rights. In 1958 Cesar became head of the CSO.

Fred Ross and Cesar worked together for the CSO.

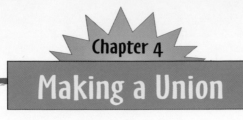

In 1962, Cesar started a union for migrant workers. Then he got a great idea. He asked people not to buy any grapes until the workers made more money. Many people stopped buying grapes. The farm owners gave in.

This girl helped tell people about Cesar's idea: Don't buy grapes.

Later, Cesar started a new union. Cesar's union got California to pass a new work law. Migrant farm workers now have the same rights as other workers.

Cesar Chavez died on April 23, 1993. His hard work made life better for migrant farm workers.

This is Cesar's grandson, also named Cesar Chavez. He is standing in front of a picture of his grandfather.

Timeline

1927—Cesar Estrada Chavez is born near Yuma, Arizona.

1938—The Chavez family loses their farm. They move to California and become migrant farm workers.

1945—Cesar joins the Navy.

1948—Cesar marries Helen Fabela.

1952—Cesar meets Fred Ross and goes to work for the CSO.

1962—Cesar founds the National Farm Workers Association.

1965—Cesar tells people not to buy grapes until the workers are paid fairly.

1974—California passes a law giving farm workers many rights.

1993—Cesar Chavez dies in Arizona.

Learn More

Books

Herrera, Juan Felipe. *The Upside Down Boy/El Nino de Cabeza.* San Francisco: Children's Book Press, 2000.

Krull, Kathleen. *Harvesting Hope: The Story of Cesar Chavez.* San Diego, Calif.: Harcourt, Inc., 2003.

Roman, Michelle. *Becoming Cesar Chavez.* Fresno, Calif.: Poppy Lane, 2001.

Internet Addresses

Cesar E. Chavez Foundation

<http://www.cesarechavezfoundation.org>

Cesar E. Chavez Model Curriculum (for teachers)

<http://www.cde.ca.gov/cesarchavez>

Index